SITUATIONAL JUDGMENT MASTERY

100+ Workplace Scenarios
& Expert Strategies

Copyright 2025 Complete Test Preparation Inc. All Rights Reserved.

No part of this book may be reproduced or transferred in any form or by any means, graphic, electronic, or mechanical, including photocopying, recording, web distribution, taping, or by any information storage retrieval system, without the written permission of the author.

Notice: Complete Test Preparation Inc. makes every reasonable effort to obtain from reliable sources accurate, complete, and timely information about the tests covered in this book. Nevertheless, changes can be made in the tests or the administration of the tests at any time and Complete Test Preparation Inc. makes no representation or warranty, either expressed or implied as to the accuracy, timeliness, or completeness of the information contained in this book. Complete Test Preparation Inc. make no representations or warranties of any kind, express or implied, about the completeness, accuracy, reliability, suitability or availability with respect to the information contained in this document for any purpose. Any reliance you place on such information is therefore strictly at your own risk.

The author(s) shall not be liable for any loss incurred as a consequence of the use and application, directly or indirectly, of any information presented in this work. Sold with the understanding, the author is not engaged in rendering professional services or advice. If advice or expert assistance is required, the services of a competent professional should be sought.

The company, product and service names used in this publication are for identification purposes only. All trademarks and registered trademarks are the property of their respective owners. Complete Test Preparation Inc. is not affiliated with any educational institution.

We strongly recommend that students check with exam providers for up-to-date information regarding test content.

Complete Test Preparation Inc. is not affiliated with the Canada Federal Government, nor the Public Service Commission, who are not involved in the production of, and do not endorse this publication.

ISBN-13: 9781772455250

Version 9 June 2025

About Complete Test Preparation Inc.

Why Us?
The Complete Test Preparation Team has been publishing high quality study materials since 2005, with a catalogue of over 145 titles, in English, French and Chinese, as well as ESL curriculum for all levels.

To keep up with the industry changes, we update everything all the time!

And the best part?
With every purchase, you're helping people all over the world improve themselves and their education. So thank you in advance for supporting this mission with us! Together, we are truly making a difference in the lives of those often forgotten by the system.

Charities that we support -
https://www.test-preparation.ca/charities-and-non-profits/

You have definitely come to the right place.
If you want to spend your valuable study time where it will help you the most - we've got you covered today and tomorrow.

Published by
Complete Test Preparation Inc.
Victoria BC Canada

Visit us on the web at https://www.test-preparation.ca
Printed in the USA

Feedback

We welcome your feedback. Email us at feedback@test-preparation.ca with your comments and suggestions. We carefully review all suggestions and often incorporate reader suggestions into upcoming versions. As a Print on Demand Publisher, we update our products frequently.

Contents

6 GETTING STARTED

10 PRACTICE TEST QUESTIONS SET 1
Answer Key   41

55 PRACTICE TEST QUESTIONS SET 2
Answer Key   85

95 CONCLUSION

97 ONLINE RESOURCES

Getting Started

CONGRATULATIONS! By deciding to take a Situational Judgement test, you have taken the first step toward a great future! Of course, there is no point in taking this important examination unless you intend to do your best to earn the highest grade you possibly can. That means getting yourself organized and discovering the best approaches, methods and strategies to master the material. Yes, that will require real effort and dedication, but if you are willing to focus your energy and devote the study time necessary, before you know it you will be opening that letter of acceptance.

We know that taking on a new endeavour can be scary, and it is easy to feel unsure of where to begin. That's where we come in. This study guide is designed to help you improve your test-taking skills, show you a few tricks of the trade and increase both your competency and confidence.

What is a Situational Judgement Test?

Situational Judgement tests (SJT) give test candidates realistic, hypothetical scenarios and ask the individual to choose the most appropriate response or to rank the responses according to the most effective. SJTs can be pencil and paper, computer based, films, or audio. Situational Judgement tests are multiple choice.

Situational Judgement Tests (SJT) generally cover the following areas in the given scenarios:

- Communication
- Being a Team Player
- Building Relationships
- Organization and Planning
- Focus on Customer
- Analytical and Creative Thinking

Situational Judgement

This section contains Situational Judgement practice questions. So, while the self-assessment contains general questions similar to the situational judgement questions likely to be on most tests, but are not intended to be identical to the exam questions.

Situational judgement questions test your judgement, not what you memorize. The best way to study for this type of question is to practice, using your best judgement.

The questions below are not the same as you will find on your test - that would be too easy! And nobody knows what the questions will be and they change all the time. Mostly the changes consist of substituting new questions for old, but the changes can be new question formats or styles, changes to the number of questions in each section, changes to the time limits for each section and combining sections. So, while the format and exact wording of the questions may differ slightly, and change from year to year, if you can answer the questions below, you will have no problem with the situational judgement section on your test.

Situational Judgement Self-Assessment

Situational Judgement Tests generally cover the following areas in the given scenarios:

- Communication
- Being a Team Player
- Building Relationships

- Organization and Planning
- Focus on the Customer
- Analytical and Creative Thinking

Once complete, use the table below to assess your understanding of the content, and prepare your study schedule described in chapter 1.

80% - 100%	Excellent – you have mastered the content!
60 – 79%	Good. You have a working knowledge. Even though you can just pass this section, you may want to review the Tutorials and do some extra practice to see if you can improve your mark.
40% - 59%	Below Average. You do not understand Situational judgement problems. Review the tutorials, and retake this quiz again in a few days, before proceeding to the rest of the study guide.
Less than 40%	Poor. You have a very limited understanding of Situational judgement problems. Please review the Tutorials, and retake this quiz again in a few days, before proceeding to the rest of the study guide.

Practice Test Questions Set 1

The questions below are not the same as you will find on a situational judgement test - that would be too easy! And nobody knows what the questions will be and they change all the time. Below are general questions that cover the same subject areas as most situational judgement tests. So, while the format and exact wording of the questions may differ slightly, and change from year to year, if you can answer the questions below, you will have no problem with your situational judgement test.

For the best results, take these practice test questions as if it were the real exam. Set aside time when you will not be disturbed, and a location that is quiet and free of distractions. Read the instructions carefully, read each question carefully, and answer to the best of your ability.

Use the bubble answer sheets provided. When you have completed the Practice Questions, check your answer against the Answer Key and read the explanation provided.

Do not attempt more than one set of practice test questions in one day. After completing the first practice test, wait two or three days before attempting the second set of questions.

Answer Sheet

1. A B C D
2. A B C D
3. A B C D
4. A B C D
5. A B C D
6. A B C D
7. A B C D
8. A B C D
9. A B C D
10. A B C D
11. A B C D
12. A B C D
13. A B C D
14. A B C D
15. A B C D
16. A B C D
17. A B C D
18. A B C D
19. A B C D
20. A B C D
21. A B C D
22. A B C D
23. A B C D
24. A B C D
25. A B C D
26. A B C D
27. A B C D
28. A B C D
29. A B C D
30. A B C D
31. A B C D
32. A B C D
33. A B C D
34. A B C D
35. A B C D
36. A B C D
37. A B C D
38. A B C D
39. A B C D
40. A B C D
41. A B C D
42. A B C D
43. A B C D
44. A B C D
45. A B C D
46. A B C D
47. A B C D
48. A B C D
49. A B C D
50. A B C D
51. A B C D
52. A B C D
53. A B C D
54. A B C D
55. A B C D
56. A B C D
57. A B C D
58. A B C D
59. A B C D
60. A B C D

Situational Judgement

Scenario 1

An editor complains about your work regardless of how much you try. How should you deal with a difficult supervisor?

    a. Ignore his negative comments and stay positive

    b. Listen attentively to the criticism and try to comply.

    c. Refer to the company's policy document for further information.

    d. Blame the supervisor for being ignorant.

Scenario 2

Workload is increasingly becoming a problem in your department. How should you work to improve the situation?

    a. Assign more work to a junior employees as well as divide the work more efficiently.

    b. Request more staff or temporary help from the management.

    c. Ask for higher pay for you and your team.

    d. Do what you can and leave what you can't.

Scenario 3

Your team goes out for a party but there is a line-up and the wait time is too long. Some of your team grow impatient and want to leave. How should you handle this situation?

    a. Offer incentives and ask them to be patient.

    b. Request patience for a little while longer.

    c. Lead them in demonstrating against the unfair treatment.

    d. Keep quiet and let things fall into place.

Scenario 4

Suppose you fail while undertaking a project given to you by your supervisor. How should you react?

    a. Freak out and blame the failure on yourself and your team.

    b. Ensure that you learn from the mistakes and move on.

    c. Ignore the failure and console yourself that failure is inevitable.

    d. None of the above.

Scenario 5

You have been given an assignment together with a colleague. When you need crucial information, your colleague takes too long time to respond. What should you do?

    a. Discuss with your colleague and see if there is a solution.

    b. Discuss the matter with your immediate supervisor.

    c. Demand that he keeps you posted at all times and respond faster.

    d. Acquire information from other sources on your own.

Scenario 6

The company you work for undergoes various changes. You, and some of the employees, are finding it hard to adjust to rapid and constant changes. How should you act in such a situation?

a. Rebel against the proposed changes.

b. Read new company books to improve yourself.

c. Mobilize other employees to attend training.

d. Become more actively involved in the changes.

Scenario 7

As a team leader, your company assigns you with a huge project. What are the first steps you should take?

a. Explain the project and goals to everyone.

b. Involve only the people you deem important to avoid confusion.

c. Ask for assistance from the experienced supervisors.

d. Decline any assistance from anybody who may deter your project.

Scenario 8

You are in charge of a team that looks up to you for many things not just on work related issues. You learn some very bad news which needs to be delivered to your team. How should you go about it?

a. Be straight forward and direct.

b. Avoid addressing issues that could be unwelcome to the team.

c. Bring them together and explain as much as possible. Address their concerns.

d. Ask someone else to deliver the bad news on your behalf.

Scenario 9

You notice that your team members are actively competing against each other on a project you are overseeing. How should you react?

a. Discourage any sort of competition.

b. Monitor the competition to ensure that it's healthy and productive towards achieving the goals.

c. Allow unregulated competition where the smartest wins.

d. Offer a reward for the most productive.

Scenario 10

You face a lot of criticism at work for something you did. This weighs you down and affects your general performance. What should you do?

a. Find areas to criticize those criticizing you.

b. Let the matter be addressed by your supervisors.

c. Resent the critic.

d. Work on improving the aspect criticized by my colleagues.

Scenario 11

After working on a project for several months, it becomes clear to you that reorganizing the team is inevitable in realizing the project's vision. What should you do?

a. Discard the current team and form another.

b. Match the strengths of the team members with the overall goals stipulated.

c. Remove the less skilled employees and replace them with more experienced ones.

d. Do nothing.

Scenario 12

Some of the junior employees in your company are not under your jurisdiction yet their co-operation is important for the success of your business. How should you handle the situation?

    a. Demand for cooperation from them.

    b. Call them to a meeting and stress on the fact that you are a boss and they need to cooperate.

    c. Clearly communicate your ideas and be open to feedback.

    d. Request their supervisors to order them to cooperate with your department.

Scenario 13

You are the manger in given line of production. John, a junior employee, disregards your orders. How should you handle the situation?

    a. Request that the employee is fired immediately.

    b. Set an example by disciplining the rogue employee.

    c. Hear out and understand the reason for his disagreement.

    d. Change the directive.

Scenario 14

New facts come to your attention mid-way through a project. They require you to change most or all of your plan. How do you go about changing the decisions already made?

    a. Always keep clear communication between and among the members of the team.

    b. Abruptly change the initial plan.

    c. Consult with others on what needs to be done.

    d. Disregard the new facts.

Scenario 15

One of your employees disagrees with you concerning a new business plan. How do you go about formulating and presenting your argument without hurting them?

    a. Rebuke the employee for disobedience

    b. Over-rule the objections.

    c. Base your argument on objective facts and listen to their side of the argument.

    d. Call for disciplinary action against the employee.

Scenario 16

An agent has worked tirelessly with other company agents with no success. This client is then referred to you for assistance. How should you go about assisting the client?

    a. Refer the client to another agent who is more competent.

    b. Refuse to accept the client.

    c. Listen attentively to the issue troubling the client and offer professional assistance as you deem best.

    d. Attend to the client similar to how he has been attended in the past.

Scenario 17

The company you are working for has experienced communication hiccups and misunderstandings in the past. How should you prevent similar incidents in the future?

    a. Encourage all employees to use written communication.

    b. Make clarifications where needed and encourage team members to do the same.

    c. Refuse to consider any verbal communication.

    d. Be complacent in communicating with others.

Scenario 18

A workmate is very mean to you. You disregard this but the issue has recently been putting a lot pressure on you. You need to stay positive and motivated. How should you handle this?

    a. Become mean to them as well.

    b. Confront his ill behavior.

    c. Involve supervisors in resolving the conflict.

    d. Keep on motivating yourself to become better.

Scenario 19

A client walks into your office requesting assistance with a product. Since you are less involved in this area, you cannot help him. How should you handle the situation?

    a. Refer the client to the correct department.

    b. Welcome the client and be as hospitable as possible as you find the right person to assist him.

    c. Find the correct information and assist the client.

    d. Inform the client that the areas requested is outside your scope.

Scenario 20

A client you have been serving becomes impatience with the process. She goes out looking for the manager saying that you are taking too long to give her the assistance.

What should you do to diffuse the situation?

    a. Refuse to attend the client.

    b. Take this matter to your supervisor.

    c. Explain the process to the client why it is taking longer.

    d. Ignore the client completely.

Scenario 21

You work as a consultant in an audit firm with five co-workers in your team reporting to a team manager who reports to a department manager.

Matt, a co-worker you share an office with, requires your advice on a report he is about to present the weekly team meeting. Your team manager leads the meetings but the department manager is present usually.

Although the part of the report Matt shows you looks fine, you observe missing conclusions of the numerical analysis of a different section of the report. This does not meet the required standards of your departmental supervisor.

Matt looks confident about the part of the report and does not seem interested in your opinion.

What should you do?

> a. There is not much you can do if he is not interested in your opinion. You let it go and let him face the consequences of presenting an incomplete report.
>
> b. Notify the management if he is not keen on listening to you. Talk to your manager and let him explain to Matt why the changes are necessary.
>
> c. Put in the necessary effort to make him listen. This may be a little uncomfortable, but you explain the reasons behind your criticism hoping Matt will understand.
>
> d. Try to educate him by showing him proper reports and company policy.

Scenario 22

You are working as a management trainee in a leisure company and are currently placed at a busy leisure club in the city center. You get a call from head office that a small leisure club has an abnormally large number of staff on off due to sickness today. You are requested by head office to spend time at that leisure club as the manager is off and his deputy is on holiday. However, you have a pile of paperwork and several meetings with your team at your club.

What should you do?

> a. Explain your situation and inquire from the head office contact how you are supposed to prioritize your day.
>
> b. Suggest that you are given 30 minutes to reschedule your day and promise to give them a response after half an hour.
>
> c. Since you are busy suggest that they call other nearby clubs to find a manager who might be able to step in to help the understaffed club.
>
> d. Agree to spend time at the understaffed club but take your paperwork with you.

Scenario 23

You have been a graduate trainee with the government for close to six months. You joined the program with 3 trainees that you have been working with closely on several projects. You notice one of your colleagues has not been usual for a while.

You also over-hear your manager say she was not impressed by his contribution during a customer meeting. You and this colleague are supposed to jointly deliver work for a customer the following week. You think he will not be able to deliver successfully.

What should you do?

a. Take him for coffee and ask him how he is doing and express your concern that you are worried he has not been himself lately.

b. Take him aside and explain to him that you can tell he is not functioning to his level best and offer to take up majority of the work on the following weeks project.

c. Monitor him closely for a while, and intentionally find ways to work with him more closely.

d. Approach your manager and let him know that you overheard him talk about your colleague. Let him know that you also think there are some problems.

Question 24

You hold a position as a graduate trainee position at a global bank branch. You have been requested by your manager to recommend options that will increase opportunities for business development within the branch. Several initiatives have been put in place to offers\ solutions for small businesses with little success. The team has been trained on the solutions and other branches have had success marketing them in their areas. The team in your branch is responsible for selling these packages with individual targets in place.

What should you do?

a. Talk to colleagues in branches that have been more successful and ask them what they are doing to be successful in their efforts to sale these packages.

b. Run another short training about the packages to the branch members responsible for selling them to customers.

c. Suggest that you come up with a free networking event for local businesses one evening at a nearby hotel.

d. Suggest you can call several local businesses to discuss the offer and try to close some sales personally.

Scenario 25

You noticed there is a lot of useful research conducted for clients while working as a graduate trainee for a consulting firm. You can see that clients and colleagues would benefit from this but there is no clear method to disseminate this. You discuss it the manager and suggest ways to make the practice even better.

What should you do?

> a. Propose that you have a webinar every 90 days where key players in the company share findings from their research with others.
>
> b. Suggest a two-day internal conference every year that focusses on sharing research findings among employees.
>
> c. Suggest an area is created on the company internal network where employees are encouraged to share what they discover from their research.
>
> d. Suggest the company sets up a research forum with the purpose of ensuring the research findings are shared in the company with departmental representatives from all departments.

Scenario 26

You work as a trainee in a large bank. An upset client calls while you are working in the customer service department. He claims he has not received a refund on some fees he was charged in error. He claims one of your colleagues promised the money would be in his account today but has not yet arrived. He is getting upset and is raising his voice.

What would you say?

a. "If you give me your account details, I will do all I can to investigate what happened."

b. "Let me talk to the colleague you mentioned to get to the bottom of this. Please hold on a couple of minutes I will talk to him and get back to you."

c. "I understand that you are upset but please calm down so that I can help you."

d. "I believe there is a good reason for this. Give your account details so I can investigate."

Scenario 27

You are working in an electronics company as a trainee and are part of an international project looking at new marketing opportunities. You find it difficult to understand what a colleague is saying during a conference call. She is also a graduate trainee and during your interactions on other calls you have got on well. She has a strong accent and speaks very quickly when she is nervous. You are in the meeting room with several colleagues and the project lead. You can see that your colleagues are also having a difficult time understanding her.

What should you do?

a. When she is no longer speaking, send her a private message explaining to her that she should slow down a little as several people are finding it difficult to understand her.

b. Discuss your concerns after the call to other team members and suggest you compare notes to ensure you are on the same page.

c. Mention your concerns to the project lead after the call and offer to talk to your colleague since you have a working relationship.

d. Call your colleague after the call and ask how she finds the project. Politely mention that you find it difficult to understand what she says at times and suggest that slowing down would help.

Scenario 28

You submitted a paper to an upcoming professional global conference. You have attended the conference before and have met people from your industry and universities around the world. The paper has a summary of a research you conducted and believe it will be helpful. You learned that the paper has been accepted and you have been asked by your manager to find a way to present the paper that will make the biggest impact. You have limited time for your presentation.

How do you respond?

 a. Say you will employ the use of graphics and images to draw out key messages.

 b. Say you will create a presentation that reflects the research with similar section headers.

 c. Ask the manager what they think would be the best approach from their experience.

 d. Say that you will take time introducing the research approach but take most of the time talking about your findings and conclusions.

Scenario 29

You operate a 10-person group. You have professional and cooperative workers. However, you have recently found that they are taking longer breaks and work generally has been declining. You are pleased that the workplace has a nice environment, yet you are concerned with its effect on the jobs of your team.

How should you respond?

 a. Announce that any employee wanting to take a break must first ask you about that.

 b. Announce that only one worker should have a coffee break at any specified moment.

 c. Speak to the staff regarding the situation and ask for cooperation.

d. Warn team members with the deadlines and suggest there will be consequences.

Scenario 30

You feel some changes are needed after reading a study prepared by one of your team. When discussing the study with her, she disagrees with several of your statements and feels it is a stronger report at present.

What are you going to do?

    a. Explain why your opinion more thoroughly.

    b. Let her realize that your choices are final, but display empathy to her effort.

    c. Tell her it is her job, and you value her view. Your feedback will support her, and she will be able to approve or deny it.

    d. Politely invite her to object to and clarify your remarks.

Scenario 31

You are asked to prepare a presentation for your staff, with the help of your co-worker, Daniel. Your boss will make the presentation to the board of directors for approval. Daniel manages the data collection department. He is tasked with collecting data while you convert the data into PowerPoint slides. Daniel has gathered data from a paper that was incorrect - this has led you to create 30 misleading slides.

On the day you have the briefing, the supervisor counts on you to have everything ready with a lot more to do.

What is the best way to respond?

    a. Describe to the boss how Daniel gathered the data and why it took a long time. Ask Daniel if he can fix the error he made- much of it was his own.

    b. Let the boss know that you and Daniel got the data incorrect while putting together the presentation. Modify the introduction slides.

c. Do not call attention to this error. Give him handwritten notes during class with corrections to use while presenting.

d. Do not annoy the boss about this anymore. You can notify Daniel right away about changing the faulty slides.

Scenario 32

Bob is new to the office staff. Your superior, has assigned you to teach Bob the computer system due to your experience. It is a relatively simple system, however, Bob is finding it difficult to understand.

What should you do?

a. Tell him it should be easy for everyone to understand and he needs to learn it quickly.

b. Allow Anna, who has more experience than you, to conduct the lesson. Return to your other activities for the rest of the day.

c. Tell Bob to do it later. You become irritable and have to complete other tasks.

d. Discuss with Bob the issues he is having with the system. Start a new training session at a much simpler level.

Scenario 33

A client calls and criticizes you for not delivering a product by the deadline. You lookup the order and see the delivery is late due to a shortage.

What should you tell the client?

a. "I apologize; your order is delayed due to a shortage. Would you like me call when it is dispatched? "

b. "I am afraid we seem to be out of stock at the moment, but I'm certain your package will be delivered soon."

c. "The shipment has not yet been shipped; you are correct. We are out of stock right now, but I cannot do anything about that."

d. "I am afraid; this commodity seems to be out of stock now. For a while, you'll have to be careful."

Scenario 34

The store has just received a new brand of cell phone. Before marketing this new phone, which of the following is the most critical as a sales representative?

a. Ensure the new phone is appropriately displayed in the shop.

b. Estimate the new product's impact on thew market.

c. Review how competitors portray the new phone.

d. Test the commodity yourself and get acquainted with it.

Scenario 35

You work in department that shares office space with others. Everyone in your department is given a new computer system and you are left out.

What should you do?

a. Consider this as a small mistake and talk to the head of department.

b. Confront the head of department and ask him to explain why you are being treated unfairly.

c. Take a new computer from a colleague.

d. Make a complaint with the HR department.

Scenario 36

You have the knowledge that company property has been going missing for some time now. You noticed a colleague putting small things from the office in her handbag several times and suspect she is responsible.

What should you do?

>a. Find ways to get more evidence or catch her in the act.
>
>b. Face your colleague and ask her about what you have noticed then inform your manager of your suspicion.
>
>c. Raise the issue in a meeting and mention that you suspect your colleague.
>
>d. Don't do anything. Your colleague will be caught if she is guilty.

Scenario 37

After a busy day at work, you send an email with confidential information to a client by mistake.

What should you do?

>a. Leave the office and handle the matter the following day.
>
>b. Overlook the mistake, re-send the email to the correct address.
>
>c. Immediately contact the wrong recipient via phone or email to explain the mistake. Then send the email to the right person.
>
>d. Explain to your manager what happened and let them handle the matter.

Scenario 38

A patient suffering from a complex medical condition dies after a long period of treatment. Although there is enough evidence to fill a death certificate, your consultant is keen on taking a postmortem to investigate the death. The family consents to his request. However, the family speaks to you and claims they were coerced into making the decision and not happy.

What should you do?

    a. Send the family back to the consultant and ask him to speak to them again.

    b. Talk to your consultants and find out his reasons for the postmortem.

    c. Request another senior colleague to meet with the family and discuss their concerns.

    d. Personally, talk to the family about their concerns.

Scenario 39

Which action should be avoided when listening to an upset customer describing a problem?

    a. Listen carefully to the customer describing the problem.

    b. Politely requesting the customer to calm down that you can offer your assistance.

    c. Directing the customer to your supervisor.

    d. Putting effort on focusing the customer to their original need.

Scenario 40

You walk into the washroom and find a colleague crying. What should you do?

    a. Walk out and give them peace.

    b. Find the manager and leave the situation to them.

    c. Ask whether they are fine and if there is anything you can do to help.

    d. Give them a hug at tell them everything will be okay.

Scenario 41

You have assigned your team some work with a tight deadline which, unless met, means that the company is going to incur huge losses. You assign Jackie is to lead the team delivering the assignment. Two days before the deadline, Jackie shows up in your office and explains to you that it will not be possible to deliver the project on time because one of the team members failed to play his part.

How are you going to handle the situation?

    a. Quarrel with Jackie and blame the delay on her entirely as a team leader.

    b. Brainstorm with her on what may be done

    c. Ensure that both Jackie and the employee get a salary cut

    d. Call a meeting and shame the entire team for failing.

Scenario 42

A customer calls in with a list of complaints about your company. The sales representative directs the client to your office. The customer is angry and dissatisfied with their purchases.

How do you communicate to the dissatisfied customer?

a. Explain to the customer why they are wrong and how right your argument is

b. Listen carefully to the complaint without interrupting, show empathy and understanding and offer the best assistance you can.

c. Blame the customer for not reading the terms and conditions of purchase

d. Deny a refund and refer the customer to another company.

Scenario 43

A lot of shipments have been directed to your department which is currently short-staffed. The supervisor asks all employees to take turns working overtime to handle the situation. You feel worn-out having worked late more than once during the week. You and your friends have plans to go out on Friday evening but your supervisor asks you to cover for a sick colleague.

How should you respond?

a. Explain to the supervisor that those plans are hard to change because you waited two summers to re-unite with your college friends.

b. Accept the work and turn your friends down.

c. Ignore the order and go out anyway.

d. Communicate with your team members and supervisor and weigh the issues at hand and act accordingly.

Scenario 44

You have been working with a company for more than three years. During this period, you have familiarized yourself with all polices governing the company's operations. On this particular day, your immediate supervisor asks you to undertake a task which definitely goes against company policies.

What should you do?

> a. Do as the supervisor asks and disregard the company policies
>
> b. Decline to do what the supervisor asks of you.
>
> c. Explain to the supervisor that the action goes against the policies
>
> d. Ask the supervisor whether he knows the policies of the company

Scenario 45

You are working on a task that calls for skills that you don't have. You need help from your work mates who have the required skills.

How would you go about seeking collaboration?

> a. Make a thorough analysis of all the parameters at play and act decisively.
>
> b. Ask for collaboration from other team members.
>
> c. Act immediately without thinking.
>
> d. Fail to take any action.

Scenario 46

One project assigned to you involves a client, Jane. She keeps calling you to make changes to the original plan. It is your feeling that she is changing most of the projects specifics which could directly impact the budget.

How should you deal with this situation?

    a. Propose that she makes all changes in an official manner, through letters and email.

    b. Take her orders and do as she pleases to ensure customer satisfaction.

    c. Refuse to do what she asks outside of the initial contract/agreement/project.

    d. Discuss this matter with your superiors and find a way forward.

Scenario 47

A client is very much opposed to your point of view while trying to explain something to him. It is important that they are convinced about the idea you are putting across.

How would you go about making the client see things from your perspective?

    a. Begin with understanding and seeing things in your client's perspective.

    b. Begin with explaining your point of view to the client in clear and simple terms.

    c. Decode what your client could be thinking about

    d. Sit the client down and prove to him why he is wrong

Scenario 48

Conflict in the workplace is common in most organizations. Your co-worker falsely accuses you and you feel resentment towards him. The two of you get into an extended conflict and antagonistic relationship, which could see production affected.

How should you handle this situation?

    a. Apologize to your coworker.

    b. Have a supervisor involved in resolving the conflict.

    c. Act normal and pretend that nothing wrong will happen.

    d. Ask for an apology from your friend.

Scenario 49

You are on shift and performing your normal duties, when something very urgent comes up. The issue is extremely demanding and none of your colleagues have handled this type of situation before.

How should you handle this situation?

    a. Make a thorough analysis of all the parameters at play and act decisively.

    b. Ask for collaboration from other team members on the appropriate course of action.

    c. Act immediately without thinking

    d. Fail to take any action

Scenario 50

It's a bright Monday morning and you show up to work as usual. Before you get to the main door, you over-hear your team members shouting and yelling at each other. It seems like a really big fight is going on. It's obvious that your coworkers disagree on some very basic principles.

How should you go about bringing cohesion to your team?

    a. Refer this matter to your supervisor

    b. Ask what could be wrong and offer advice

    c. Talk to each of the employees separately

    d. Discuss this with the entire team and ask for solutions

Scenario 51

A customer calls to change their order but you know that their previous order is nearly ready.

What should you do?

    a. Explain that you are sorry the kitchen has almost finished preparing the meal so changing their order is not possible.

    b. Let the customer know the meal is already being prepared but this change can be easily made.

    c. Tell the customer you would place a new order for them but this may take some time.

    d. Tell the customer their meal is nearly ready so they should pick out the ingredients they don't like.

Scenario 52

You have a couple celebrating their wedding anniversary invading a reserved table as their original table is in a rather noisy location. The reserved table will be needed in 15 minutes.

What should you do?

> a. Let the customer know they cannot sit on that table as it is reserved but promise them a suitable table.
>
> b. Inform the couple they can stay on that table for a maximum of 15 minutes
>
> c. Tell the couple that it is fine they can use that table and move the reservation to a different table.
>
> d. Let the couple know that the table is booked and they have to move back to their original table.

Scenario 53

You have ten occupied table but you don't want to overwhelm the kitchen with all the orders at once.

What should you do?

> a. Take drink orders first
>
> b. Approach those without drinks and take their drink orders then proceed to those with drinks to get their food ordered
>
> c. See which customer are looking to get your attention and address them first
>
> d. Approach tables with drinks to take their orders before going to the other tables.

Scenario 54

You have clients who want to pay but also have food that is ready and has to be served hot. Making clients wait for long to pay annoys them.

What should you do?

>a. Tell the customers waiting to pay that you will be with them soon and collect the food so that it doesn't turn cold

>b. See if someone else is available to collect the payment while you collect the food

>c. Take the payment as fast as possible and let the others know that their food won't take long

>d. Take some of the payments and then go to the kitchen and ensure you communicate to all customers

Scenario 55

People are randomly shouting their orders at you and it is overwhelming.

What should you do?

>a. Ask them to be quiet so that you can clearly hear their orders and ensure they are correct.

>b. Write down what you hear and read it out to ensure it is all correct.

>c. Ask them to go round the table and give their orders on after another to ensure it is correct

>d. Check if they are happy for the food to arrive at different times and write down as many orders as you hear for now.

Scenario 56

You just had a client telling their partner that the food was cold even after they assured you that everything is okay.

What should you do?

> a. Proceed with other tasks as they assured you that everything was fine.
>
> b. Go back and double check if everything is fine
>
> c. Proceed to the table and apologize to the lady that her food is cold and offer to have it warmed
>
> d. Wait to see if the customer will call you over directly as you are not sure if you heard them correctly.

Scenario 57

You have customers that are furious for waiting for 20 minutes to place their order. They have asked for the manager.

What should you do?

> a. Tell the customers you are sorry and will look for the manager to address the issue.
>
> b. Tell the customers you cannot talk to them while they are angry and send someone to talk to them when they have calmed down
>
> c. Tell the customer you are very busy and that they have been served faster than other customers around
>
> d. Tell the customers you are sorry and ask if they would like to order before talking to the manager

Scenario 58

There is a table with guest that are not yet ready to order but have children that keep shouting that they are hungry. You feel that this is bothering to other guests.

What should you do?

> a. Ask the parents if they are ready to order for the children as you can see, they are hungry.
>
> b. Ask the parents if they can control the noise as it is quite loud.
>
> c. Ask the children to be quiet as they are disturbing the entire restaurant
>
> d. You don't need to anything it is the responsibility of parents to take care of their children

Scenario 59

You have a customer that is very happy with your services and wants you to work in their hotel.

What should you do?

> a. Tell the customer you are pleased that he is happy but you are happy with your current place of work
>
> b. Tell the customer you will be happy to take the job immediately
>
> c. Tell the customer that proposal is inappropriate and you will not respond
>
> d. Tell the customer that you will inform the manager they are looking for some extra staff

Scenario 60

You just had a customer saying you are not fit for the job and you fear this is going to be obvious in your interactions with other customers.

What should you do?

> a. Try not to worry about what they think as long as you are doing your job right.
>
> b. Explain to other customers why you may be looking a bit upset.
>
> c. Maintain a positive attitude and smile to the other customers.
>
> d. Inform the customer that you have not received any complaints previously.

Answer Key

1. B

The editor is your boss and that's the way things are so if they are not happy that will mean some adjustment on your part. However, if you feel the editor is being unreasonable, you may want to talk with them. Choice C, referring to the company policy document is a possibility depending on the situation.

Choice A, ignorance is no defense in any situation in life. By ignoring to address the concerns of the clients you set a pace for failure. You are bound to lose more clients. Choice D, blaming the supervisor will only lead to more complications. Building resentment and bad publicity are sure consequences of such behavior.

2. A

Division of labor and specialization are the best ways of solving increasing workload. This gives the employees equal time to work on given tasks to ease the workload. Division of labor pro-motes innovation and invention and increases output per employee.

Choice B, may be a good idea, however management very likely has limited options to help. Choice C, asking for higher pay doesn't solve the problem. Choice D, may be a good option if, and only if all else fails.

3. B

You are nominally in charge so it fall on you to handle the situation. However, you can't do much about the line-up. Choice B, ask for patience for a bit longer is the best choice. Choice A, offering incentives may be considered later depending on how long you wait. Choice C, and D don't do anything to diffuse the situation.

4. B

Life is sequence of lessons that start from childhood and continues in adulthood. By learning from one's mistake, you are likely to improve next time. Sometimes we succeed and sometimes we learn. Failure is a part of life and we all should embrace failure as a lesson for a better tomor-row. It may be necessary to discuss the failure and learnings with your supervisor.

Choices A, C and D do not addresses the core issue.

5. A
First, discuss it with your colleague. There may be things you are not aware of preventing them from getting information to you quickly. If this doesn't work, go to the other options.

Choice B, going to your supervisor is an option for later. Choice C, is not a great approach. Making demands is not likely to change anything. Choice D, getting information from other sources would mean that there is a disharmony between the key participants. This may be an option for later or as a last resort.

6. D
The changes are going to continue so your choice is to resist (difficult) or become more involved. Once you are more involved in why the changes are taking place they become easier to manage.

7. A
Making sure everyone understands the goals of the project gets everyone on board is the first step.

Choice B, discriminating against team members will alienate them. Asking for assistance, choice B, from others is a necessity but comes after being clear on goals and obtaining feedback. Choice D, declining assistance is not a good strategy to start.

8. A
A straightforward and direct approach is best. Sugar coating or avoiding the bad news will come back on you.

Choices B and C, avoiding the issue and blaming others will cause problems later. Choice C, getting others to related bad news will also cause problems later.

9. B
The aspect of monitoring carries the weight in this scenario. Unregulated competition could lead to unethical behaviors. Competition is healthy in any business and human encounters. By regulating the competition, the goals are likely to be met easily.

Choice A, discouraging competition loses the benefits of competition. Competition is healthy provided limits are defined and observed. Choice D, is a good choice but choice A is better. Offering a reward may come later.

10. D
Self-improvement is a continuous process and any person who can't handle feedback or criticism positively loses the opportunity to improve.

Choice A and C, retaliating against your critics or resenting, is destructive. You can't win an argument and even when you think you have, the resentment stirred in your victim works against you and your plans. Choice B, giving the matter to supervisors, may be a next step but not a good strategy initially.

11. B
Finding and correctly matching the strengths of the individual team members with those needed in the business is the most appropriate course of action. Performance analysis will assist you in determining which employee fits which position and assigning them duties in those areas.

Choices A and B, discarding or replacing members of the team and replacing would be time consuming.

12. C
Clear communication is vital in such a scenario as a first step. If this doesn't resolve the issue the other choices are next steps.

Incorrect answers B and D
Being bossy (choice B) leads to resentment. Choice D, requesting their supervisor intervene is a possible next step.

13. C

Unless you are able to understand the reason behind the disagreement, you will not be in a position to accomplish much. By taking time to break down the details of the disagreement the chances of reaching a consensus are higher.

Terminating the employee (choice A) does not benefit the company. Choice B, disciplining is an option for later. Choice D suggests for a complete overhaul of the initial plan.

14. A
Team members need clear communication to assimilating the changes. This approach ensures that none of the team members are left behind and everyone participates mapping out the changes.

New information is to be considered and deliberated on to avoid misunderstandings. Abruptly changing or disregarding the facts will not succeed (Choices B and D). Choice C, consulting others may be necessary as a next stop.

15. C
Be objective in finding a common ground with the employee. Base your argument on facts and consider both sides of the story. Don't make accusations.

Choices A, B and D, over-ruling, rebuking or disciplining may be necessary but not as a first step.

16. C
Listening is the key to assist the client. This way you have a chance of understanding the concerns raised by the client. You will also be in a better position to close a sale.

Choice A, referring the client to another agent, you have lost the client and possibly their friends and relatives. You reduce their level of confidence in you and your company. Choice D, repeating what has been happening is also not likely to be of help to the client. Choice B, refusing the client may be an option if the issues are too difficult, but not as a first step.

17. A
Verbal communication is not always the best because there is never proof of communication. The best way to communicate is through written communication. By following written communication, you are provided with evidence of communication for reference in future.

Choice B, refusing to consider verbal communication is too extreme. Choice D is incorrect be-cause you don't want to be complacent when communicating with others.

18. C
Some of the disagreements require input from higher authority. Supervisors are in a better position to resolve a conflict between junior employees.

Choice A is not a resolution. Choice B, confronting the behavior may work if done properly, but could also make the situation worse, however, choice C is the better choice. Choice D, motivating yourself could work towards making you feel better but not towards resolving the conflict.

19. B
Choice B is the best choice. Being hospitable and polite is key.

Directing the client to other unknown offices could confuse him and you miss an opportunity. Choice C, finding the right information may seem a good choice, however, the client should be referred to an expert and knowledgeable person.

20. C
Clear communication is the best choice.
Choice B, taking this matter to the authority may make a person appear incompetent and unable to handle simple situations. Choice D is incorrect since customer satisfaction should always be a top concern.

21. A
You have tried to help, and that is the best that you can do. Choice B, notifying the management seems excessive at this point. Choice D, trying to educate him is using up your time

and effort, and since he doesn't seem receptive, probably a waster of time.

22. A
As an employee you are supposed to be flexible and be ready to help when needed. As much the management trainee is held up by other responsibilities explaining the situation to head office might help as his meetings can be rescheduled and the deadlines on the paperwork extended.

23. A
Talking to him will let him know that people care about him. He might be able to open up and talk about the challenges he is facing. Venting might help him relax and focus on his work better. Remember you aren't a counsellor but a friend and co-worker and this is a casual conversation.

24. A
Speaking to colleagues of other branches that have been successful is the best solution. Learning from the successful branches will save you wasted energy and time. Other choices, such as choice C, a networking event, or choice D, calling customers personally are good second steps.

25. D
Choice D gives the company a continuous way of sharing research findings. Creating a research forum will give employees a chance to discuss all matters research as much as they want in the forum. Having people from different departments will mean they can be able to share ideas and expertise constantly.

26. A
By choosing response A the client will be assured that their issue will be taken care of. This response makes no superficial promises, and no blame is shifted to the bank or the other colleague.

27. D
Calling her after the call will enable you maximize on the good relationship you already have and she will probably be more receptive. Politely mentioning that you find it difficult to understand her will be helpful as she might not be aware

that her accent affects, her communication and slowing down will be a good solution provided. This choice does not escalate the situation as discussing with other team member (choice B) as well as the project lead (choice C).

28. C
The manager, from their experience, will have ideas on the best way to present the material with the greatest impact. Asking for his guidance will enable you tap into his experience and make an impactful presentation.

29. C
Your workers' self-discipline is lacking and is presently harming their performance. You understand your team's good qualities and want to protect it but are still anxious about the potential of your team. Team members are friendly and have demonstrated particularly good success in the past, so appealing to their collaboration is most likely to produce results. This direct contact demonstrates the capacity to efficiently connect and control workers and to effectively use methods to improve efficiency. This approach aims to promote employee growth and development.

Introducing targets and pushing them may be a feasible tactic. It is a good form of rising efficiency. Nevertheless, this reaction often involves a punitive measure, which is too early to pursue.

30. D
Response D will be the one that encourages a genuine debate. This answer gives you more details, and you can consider together with your employee in a clear exchange of views (decision making - taking staff input). This reply demonstrates that you value the viewpoint of your staff while respecting and retaining your own opinion. It is the safest option. Different situations require different approaches to authority - in some roles; you must be stern.

In contrast, in others, an approach to instructional oversight is favored (as a guide). Choice D is the best option because it indicates that you care about your subordinates' input in the decision-making phase.

31. B

Selecting choice B, demonstrates responsibility and acceptance of the effects of one's actions. Daniel was more responsible than you for making the mistake. However, by sharing that responsibility with your teammate, you show that you are a team player (teamwork). Suppose you let your boss know that you have made a mistake. In that case, you are showing that you are responsible and have the integrity of admitting your mistakes – thus allowing your boss to be considerate of the possibility of being late for the deadline.

When you and your team work together to add an amendment to the document organically, it allows you to perfect your submission on time.

Choice A may sound like the right solution because Daniel is responsible for the issue. However, you are not prepared to divide the guilt, so you are dropping all the burden on Daniel and not offering to work together on fixing the issue. Besides, you can unintentionally harm his reputation with the boss by attacking Daniel behind his back— as he should be offered a chance to clarify.

32. A

It is the only approach when you search for the root of Bob's issues. Understanding what he finds challenging, you are showing strong listening skills. You often demonstrate adaptability by adjusting the solution to the issue. By being supportive and providing answers, you are a team player to improve the understanding of your colleague.

It might be more beneficial to let another worker with more expertise take over. However, your boss has assigned you this assignment, and it is not your duty to assign it to anyone else. Most likely, the issue does not rely on the degree of expertise but the method of teaching. You do not demonstrate the adaptability of your method of teaching by letting Anna teach him.

33. A

This answer is clear and direct.
Choice A starts by apologizing. The response given in this reply option adds an invitation to contact the customer, giving additional service and explaining operation and service

guidance.
Choice C understands the customer's concern but has no constructive effort ("I cannot do anything"), giving the appearance you are not accountable for the issue.

34. D
This question assesses how you navigate the transition to marketing a new product (adaptability). The most important approach is to familiarize yourself with the product by checking it yourself (choice D). As a sales agent, you need to be comfortable when showing it to customers.

In choices A, B, and C
It is necessary to ensure that the product display is attractive and appropriate (choice A) but not critical. It is interesting to read the product's success (choice B), which may help with your sales, but not critical. It is important and may be useful, to see what competitors are doing, (choice C) but also not critical.

35. A
Choice A is the best response. If you have not been given the right tools and equipment to do your job, talking to your head of department or direct supervisor is the right move. It is the responsibility of your head of department to help ensure you have all it takes to do your job.

Jumping to conclusions that you have been treated unfairly or taking a new colleague's computer may prove embarrassing if it was a simple mistake.

36. B
This is the right thing to do as it will give you the chance to discuss the matter with your colleague first and clear ambiguity. It is also your responsibility to report the matter to your manager.

37. C
This is the right thing to do. Explaining the mistake to the client will help protect the integrity of the message then send the email to the right person.
This is assuming the contents of the email is not catastrophic! Otherwise choice D may be appropriate.

38. B
As a professional you need to find out more about why your colleague insists on having the postmortem before anything else. This will help when talking to the family as you will be able to provide professional counsel. Your partner may have genuine concerns that need to be addressed.

39. A
Choice B should be avoided because by asking the customer to calm down instead of helping them to do so you are indirectly telling them they lack self-control. You will sound impatient and rude. Choice C, referring to the supervisor may give the customer the impression of giving them the runaround.

40. C
Response C is appropriate as shows that you have empathy. Even if you are not able to help the colleague will feel more relieved as a problem shared is a problem half solved.

41. B
What has happened in the past is hard to reverse and instead of wasting more time, a good leader would first, work towards meeting the requirements. In this given scenario, the possibility of incurring losses would be blamed on you. The most correct thing to do therefore is to brainstorm with Jackie and the rest of the team on what may be done by each member to meet the deadline.

Choices A, C and D will lead to resentment against the company and yourself and would be bad for moral. The object is to avoid loss and complete the project.

42. B
Effective communication is two-sided. Before you respond to the client's complaint, it is important to understand the complaint. Listen carefully and break down each important factor. Without proper listening, you are bound to misunderstand and irritate the client further. This way you end up losing clients. Be empathetic in your response and make yourself easy to understand.

Most people are naturally inclined to thinking that they are always correct in their thinking. This natural bias causes people to feel bad whenever they are proven wrong by someone. Choice A could seem appropriate, but it is detrimental for the future of the business. Most people blame everything on everyone but themselves. When you blame them, choice C, they are less likely to become loyal customers and your business loses in the long run. Choice D is obviously incorrect and can be eliminated right away.

43. D
Communication is very essential in any business undertaking. It is important to tell your side of the story as well as listen to deliberations by the team members. Consultations lead to better decision making.

Choice A seems appropriate; however, it fails to account for the supervisor's point of view or argument. However valid your argument might be, it is not sufficient to solve the issue. Going to work unwillingly (choice B) on the other hand is bad for you and for the company as well. You won't be able to concentrate and your productivity will be affected. Finding common ground or some type of accommodation is the best thing to do.

44. C
It is possible the supervisor is unaware of a policy. It therefore becomes important to speak with them politely.

Rarely are supervisors wrong. However sometimes unexpected things happen, but that does not allow you to do something you know violates company policy (Choice A). Declining to do the task (Choice B) without explanation is not likely to be taken well by your superior. Generally supervisors know the policies better than you although it is possible (Choice D). Choice C is the better choice.

45. B
Two heads are better than one. By allowing others to have an input in the final decision, you not only reduce unnecessary resistance but also increase employee commitment. To be effective, a leader should ensure team members are part of the decision-making process. Being involved gives them a sense of importance and belonging.

It is possible to make a thorough analysis of the factors involved in this and assume that one is able to make a decision that will be accepted by all (Choice A) however getting buy-in from everyone is a better strategy. Choices C and D are Obviously wrong choices and can be eliminated right away.

46. D
Some things are beyond your capacity as an employee, and above your pay-grade. Whether it comes from the client or from other colleagues some issues need to be forwarded to your superiors. By directing Jane to your superiors you will have drawn a line in the chain of command. You will have presented the company with appropriate information for them to make an informed decision.

You cannot accept or refuse to meet the new demands from the client as you don't have the authority (choices B and C). Communicating in an official way is important for documentation purposes. By asking the client to write letters and email, (choice A) evidence for financial accounting is availed. However, it should not stop there.

47. A
Unless you first understand the viewpoint of your client, it will be very difficult to show them otherwise. By showing the client that you understand his problem, he is much likely to agree with you at some point.

It's not possible to read the mind of the other person, at least in practice. Unless you listen to the client, decoding his thoughts will be a great challenge to you (choice C). Choice B suggests a noble solution to the problem but fails to address the fundamental aspect of listening. Choice D is not an effective strategy - nobody like to be told they are wrong.

48. B
Involving a neutral person (the supervisor) in conflict resolution leads to better understanding amongst the discontented parties. By involving a third party, you can diffuse the situation quickly and amicably. The leader offers proper guidance and issues directions to safeguard the interests of the organization.

It is not a sure thing that issuing an apology would bring to an end of the conflict (choice A) – more than that is required.

Similarly choice C, is not a solution, as it may be taken as an accusation.

49. B
The phrase, two heads are better than one is a full of psychological truth. Asking for collaboration from others gives you a better chance to analyze the situation and decide wisely. It also makes them feel valued which raises their commitment levels.

This is a good choice but choice B, asking for collaboration is better. Choices C and D, taking action without information, is dangerous to the business. It is similar to driving a car blindfolded. It is hard to make the right call when faced with a new challenge. Making decisions under pressure is a challenge to most leaders. Chances of error are so high that consulting is not an choice, but a necessity.

50. A
Work-related conflict should be resolved by higher authority. An independent supervisor can provide the appropriate direction.

Choice D, discussing as a team and asking for solutions could deteriorate with members taking sides. Involve only the right people while solving such specific problems. Choice C, talking to each separately, may resolve but you are taking a chance you will not be able to resolve. Bringing it to you superiors is the best choice (choice A). Choice B, offering unsolicited advice would not be appreciated or resolve the situation.

51. C
This takes the customer demand into consideration but also lets them know that they will have to wait longer.

52. A
This addresses the couples concerns and preserves the reserved table.

53. B
This buys time for everyone.

54. B
Delegating duties will ensure effectiveness.

55. A
This will ensure accuracy in a calm environment. The other choices just create more chaos.

56. B
This shows that you are genuinely concerned.

57. D
This shows remorse and that you seek to find a solution even before the manager arrives.

58. B
This will reduce the noise and make the other guests comfortable.

59. A
This response is both polite and professional and shows your loyalty.

60. A
This is the right thing to do as the customers attitude should not dictate your productivity. The other choices are emotional responses.

Practice Test Questions Set 2

The questions below are not the same as you will find on a situational judgement test - that would be too easy! And nobody knows what the questions will be and they change all the time. Below are general questions that cover the same subject areas as most situational judgement tests. So, while the format and exact wording of the questions may differ slightly, and change from year to year, if you can answer the questions below, you will have no problem with your situational judgement test.

For the best results, take these practice test questions as if it were the real exam. Set aside time when you will not be disturbed, and a location that is quiet and free of distractions. Read the instructions carefully, read each question carefully, and answer to the best of your ability.

Use the bubble answer sheets provided. When you have completed the Practice Questions, check your answer against the Answer Key and read the explanation provided.

Do not attempt more than one set of practice test questions in one day. After completing the first practice test, wait two or three days before attempting the second set of questions.

Answer Sheet

1. A B C D	21. A B C D	41. A B C D
2. A B C D	22. A B C D	42. A B C D
3. A B C D	23. A B C D	43. A B C D
4. A B C D	24. A B C D	44. A B C D
5. A B C D	25. A B C D	45. A B C D
6. A B C D	26. A B C D	46. A B C D
7. A B C D	27. A B C D	47. A B C D
8. A B C D	28. A B C D	48. A B C D
9. A B C D	29. A B C D	49. A B C D
10. A B C D	30. A B C D	50. A B C D
11. A B C D	31. A B C D	51. A B C D
12. A B C D	32. A B C D	52. A B C D
13. A B C D	33. A B C D	53. A B C D
14. A B C D	34. A B C D	54. A B C D
15. A B C D	35. A B C D	55. A B C D
16. A B C D	36. A B C D	56. A B C D
17. A B C D	37. A B C D	57. A B C D
18. A B C D	38. A B C D	58. A B C D
19. A B C D	39. A B C D	59. A B C D
20. A B C D	40. A B C D	60. A B C D

Scenario 1

Daniel is working on a project that seems to give him a lot of difficulty. He has shown signs of depression in the last week.

What should you do to help him out?

   a. Motivate Daniel trying to get the bottom of his issues.
   b. Inform the supervisors.
   c. Take him for some counseling sessions.
   d. Do absolutely nothing.

Scenario 2

A sales seminar you attended insists that to close more sales, you need to work on making a better first impression.

What should you do to close more sales?

   a. Dress smartly and speak clearly.
   b. Conduct business as usual.
   c. Dramatize your ideas to create rapport.
   d. Ignore the advice from the supervisor.

Scenario 3

You are working with a cross-functional team. The other team members are not keen about the recommendations you give. You are worried they may sacrifice quality to the point of jeopardizing customer privacy.

What should you do?

   a. Pick concrete issues where you feel that the project is at risk and bring them to your manager.
   b. Insist on a plan to minimize the risks you have seen.
   c. State your concerns and let the team decide on the way forward.
   d. Write a memo to the team on the potential risks so the in case of a problem you can deflect the blame.

Scenario 4

As an employee of many years at your company, you feel totally demotivated and dissatisfied with your work. You need to improve.

What are you likely to do to achieve your objectives?

    a. Find a new place to work.

    b. Find new tasks to re-engage your interest.

    c. Listen to motivational speeches.

    d. Learn to always stay positive.

Scenario 5

Some of your team members are less committed than in the recent past.

How should you go about improving commitment?

    a. Introduce work incentives.

    b. Reduce compensation for the employees who are not producing.

    c. Talk to the employees on the need of being committed.

    d. Fire the team and get another team.

Scenario 6

Sam, a 30 year-old employee in your organization has shown exemplary work. You want to praise his work in front of the other employees.

How should you go about praising him?

    a. Wait until everyone is together and compliment him.

    b. Contrast his work with the poor work of the others.

    c. Email all the employees.

    d. Ignore this idea.

Scenario 7

While working with your team members on a project you realize that things are not going well.

How should you motivate the team to perform better?

    a. Meet regularly to discuss on issues.

    b. Explain how lucky they are.

    c. Select the best team players and assign them more responsibility.

    d. Become actively involved in daily operations of the business.

Scenario 8

Most of the strategies you have adopted thus far don't seem to be working in getting team to do the right thing. You feel the need to set an example.

How should you go about this?

    a. Work twice as hard.

    b. Report to work early and leave late.

    c. Lecture the team to strive to be like you.

    d. Condemn the team for being lazy.

Scenario 9

You have formulated the goals of your department together with your team members. However, you realize that you are not yet sure on how those goals are going to be achieved.

How should you go about such a situation?

    a. Read and re-read the goals for full comprehension.

    b. Ensure team members understand what is required of them.

    c. Brainstorm on ideas that could get you to your goal.

    d. Just do the work anyhow.

Scenario 10

You are in a fast-paced environment and your job demands that you achieve a set objectives. This, according to you is a real challenge.

How should you achieve your objectives?

    a. Let the team know the deadlines to the set objectives.

    b. Keep the information to yourself.

    c. Work three times harder.

    d. Use the internet to learn more.

Scenario 11

While communicating with your juniors and superiors, you realize that several things are hindering you from staying actively engaged in the conversation.

How would you address this issue?

    a. Start practicing yoga and wellness meditation.

    b. Be keen and attentive while communicating.

    c. Listen attentively without thinking.

    d. Do not judge.

Scenario 12

You and your team encounter new challenges on a certain project. You realize the need to rally the team behind the project to get through this difficult time.

How should you achieve this?

    a. Show the team that you value their input.

    b. Be harsh to the team members.

    c. Assert your authority as a supervisor.

    d. Dictate what needs to be done during hard times.

Scenario 13

You have been assigned a new type of project. None of you are qualified to undertake the project.

How should you handle this situation?

    a. Let the team know the deadlines to the set objectives.

    b. Keep the information to yourself.

    c. Call a meeting and strategize.

    d. Use the internet to learn more.

Scenario 15

After realizing losses for some time now, your supervisor blames you and your team. However, you know for sure that it was the supervisor who is responsible for the loss.

How should you handle the situation?

    a. Blame the loss on the supervisor.

    b. Take up this matter to higher authority.

    c. Explain to the team that you are being blamed and strategize.

    d. Deny the blame.

Scenario 16

You overhear discussions during coffee break about your planned termination. However, you feel that you are being wrongfully accused.

How would you react in such a situation?

    a. Explain your side of the story.

    b. Accuse other employees.

    c. Blame the company.

    d. Accept defeat and go home.

Scenario 17

You are required to collaborate with a coworker who is tough to please. For the success of the project, both of you need to work together. What is the first step dealing with this situation?

a. Stay calm and try to understand their point of view.

b. Demean them and disregard their input.

c. Report to your supervisor that you can't work with them.

d. Ignore their unhelpful behavior.

Scenario 18

Your colleague has recently been criticized for poor performance. You need to do something to uplift their spirits.

How should you go about this?

a. Criticize his weaknesses.

b. Tell of his critics.

c. Show that you care.

d. Encourage them to learn from their mistakes.

Scenario 19

You are an employee at a company that has adopted new technology, and everyone feels uncertain and out of place. How would you go about making them feel comfortable and more productive?

a. Introduce more training.

b. Give them positive feedback.

c. Rebel against the new technology.

d. Ensure that everyone feels involved in the company.

Scenario 20

In the past, your department has been commended for excellent performance. You notice one of your team members is distracted, distressed and falling behind.

How would you address this issue?
   a. Refer him to the guidance and counseling team.
   b. Actively listen to his problems and compare them with yours.
   c. Report this matter to your supervisor.
   d. Actively listen and advise him to the best of your ability.

Scenario 21

During your morning brief, the Infection Control instructs that all staff must roll up their sleeves when having clinical interactions with patients. During your shift, your colleague has her sleeves down.

What should you do?

   a. Tell Infection Control that your colleague is not complying with their policy
   b. Speak directly to your colleague about your observation.
   c. Raise your observation with to the nurse in charge of the ward.
   d. Do not say anything immediately but monitor the situation over the course of the next few days

Scenario 22

A patient with end-stage respiratory failure that requires continuous oxygen therapy informs you that he knows he is dying and wants to die at home. He has not talked about this to anyone as he thinks it will upset his family and the nurses taking care of him.

What should you do?

> a. Tell him that he needs to stay in hospital while on oxygen.
>
> b. Tell him that the team will take account of his wishes.
>
> c. Discuss with his family his wish to die at home.
>
> d. Discuss his home circumstances with his General Practitioner.

Scenario 23

A customer calls to raise a complain that a package he had ordered had not arrived by the due date. You check the order and find it had not been delivered as the product is out of stock.

What would you say?

> a. "I apologize; we have a delay on your order. Would you like me to call you when we it has been dispatched?"
>
> b. "I'm sorry, we seem to be out of stock, but I assure you the product will be delivered soon."
>
> c. "You are right; the package has not been delivered because we are out of stock. There is nothing I can do to help."
>
> d. "I'm sorry; we are currently out of stock of this product. You will have to be patient a little longer."

Scenario 24

A new mobile phone model has been stocked in your shop.

Which of these is the most important this you should do as a sales representative before selling this new model?

    a. Ensure the product is displayed in the store prominently.

    b. Research on the popularity of the new model.

    c. Find out how the product is being presented by your competitors

    d. Try out the product personally to familiarize with it.

Scenario 25

You have a colleague that keeps asking you to check their assignment at the last minute. The colleague has asked you to help edit her assignment when you are working on a presentation. You see that this will consume the better part of your day as it needs a lot of work.

What should you do?

    a. Help with editing the document and find time to finish your presentation at night

    b. Inform the colleague that you have no time and focus on your task

    c. Let your manager know that your colleague's presentation is terrible and that you have no time to help

    d. Help the colleague this time and plan a meeting to talk about this and find a way to handle such situations in the future.

Scenario 26

Your team been working on a project for months and it is almost complete. Your team will present your work to the client in a week. You discover an error in the modeling that could change the conclusion drawn. Correcting the analysis means you will have to redo all the work but there is no time for this.

What should you do?

> a. Since no one noticed the error for such a long time ignore the error and make the presentation as it is.
>
> b. Report it to your senior and find out what can be done.
>
> c. Ask the most trusted team members to go through the material and discus what should be done.
>
> d. Call the client and invent an excuse to get an extension.

Scenario 27

You are a supervisor where one of your juniors is a close friend to your manager and talks to the manager about your projects before you get a chance to report. This embarrasses you as he exaggerates the potential risks.

What should you do?

> a. Befriend the employee and establish better ground rules
>
> b. Ask your boss to only share information with you
>
> c. Maneuver the employee into difficult situations that cause poor performance and fire them
>
> d. Isolate this employee so they have less impact on your team

Scenario 28

You are working in as a retail assistant and discover a customer has been browsing your section for a while and is visibly getting frustrated. After talking to him you discover the item, he is looking for is not available. You have to inform him the Item is out of stock.

What should you do?

a. Apologize that the item is out of stock and recommend an online retailer.

b. Offer to order the item for the customer and promise to call him when the item arrives.

c. Offer the customer the items serial number so that he can easily find it elsewhere.

d. Suggests that he tries one of your other stores that is 40 minutes' drive away.

Scenario 29

You are working in a retail store with a colleague out on off. You discover that their section of the store is untidy while you are going on your tea break.

What should you do?

a. Take your tea break and tidy it up on your way back if it remains the same

b. Go back and ask for permission from your team leader to tidy up the place

c. Do nothing as the team leader has it under control

d. Inform the team leader that there is problem in his section

Scenario 30

You have been asked to increase your sale by 15% as compared to July last year. July is a difficult month for children book sales as parents don't buy books at the end of the term.

a. Put a handwritten poster promoting your range of summer activity books for children.

b. Pick up a selection of summer-themed books and summer activity books and put them at the front of the children's area

c. Tidy up the children's book area.

d. Approach as many customers as possible with children's books and showing them the wide range of summer children's books and their location.

Scenario 31

You are working on busy day and the credit card system suddenly fails. You are informed it will take the provider 15 minutes to fix the issue. There is a long queue of customers waiting.

What should you do?

a. Inform the customers of the problem and the time it would take to solve the problem. This would save those paying by cash.

b. Continue serving the customers and apologize for the absence of the credit card payment option.

c. Ask the team leader what to do.

d. Take your afternoon break and let the customer come back later.

Scenario 32

You have been concerned about increasing signs of poor team morale amongst your team.

What should you do?

> a. Summon the team leaders separately to hear their explanations
>
> b. Leave things to settle down for a while rather than causing anyone distress
>
> c. Approach some staff from each of the teams for an informal chat
>
> d. Hold a brainstorm meeting for all team leaders to get fresh ideas

Scenario 33

As graduate trainee manager, you have discovered that none of your team objectives have been achieved.

What should you do?

> a. Use 1-on-1's to discuss effective targets and to jointly agreeing new ones.
>
> b. Scrap the objective setting idea since it clearly doesn't work.
>
> c. Mail the team an urgent request to work more closely together.
>
> d. Organize a team meeting to discuss attitudes and lack of effort being shown.

.Scenario 34

You are leading a daily huddle with your over-worked nursing team. A new, junior colleague has been regularly interrupting other team members as they voice their own problems. You think they're trying to impress their new team by monopolizing the medical answers to each problem raised.

What should you do?

    a. Tell the new nurse to stop distracting everyone from alternative solutions.

    b. Ask why your more experienced team members are not offering their own solutions.

    c. Firmly suggest to your new colleague that it's fairer to let everyone contribute.

    d. Assuming the others agree with you; state what you think is happening here.

Scenario 35

You manage a specialist customer service help desk and realize the team members are introverts and don't engage in a lot of conversations. This has led to poor team spirit and job satisfaction.

What should you do?

    a. Call a one-off emergency meeting to highlight objectives and the lack of collaboration.

    b. Start by introducing half-hour, weekly catch-up meetings for the team.

    c. Implement compulsory training courses on interpersonal skills as soon as possible.

    d. Familiarize yourself with the team objectives, then email regular updates on each one's progress.

Scenario 36

You have the responsibility to read through an intern's draft report and have discovered the report does not meet any of the objectives set. You have limited time to improve the report before presenting it to your client.

What should you do?

a. Let your intern find out what happens when a client receives a sub-standard report.

b. Forward the draft report to other analysts in your department for their own comments.

c. Ask your own manager what would have happened if you hadn't checked this report.

d. Email your collated amends to the intern; offering to explain each one in further detail.

Scenario 37

You are a busy team leader attending a meeting where the presenter has overrun the allocated time. You agree that the presentation is going on for too long.

What should you do?

a. Leave the meeting and explain you have an urgent matter to attend to.

b. Wrap up the session then set up a presentation review later.

c. Wrap-up the session by secretly messaging the whole team to ask questions.

d. Leave time management to the presenter as it is his/her responsibility.

Scenario 38

You work in a shared office next to a noisy colleague which is giving you a difficult time concentrating. No one is talking about it but you are not the only one inconvenienced.

What should you do?

> a. Refer the matter to your senior, since they have overall responsibility.
>
> b. Make even more noise than this colleague - to show them just annoying it is.
>
> c. Email your noisy colleague to complain, cc'ing in your manager.
>
> d. Talk to your noisy colleague and request more reasonable behavior.

Scenario 39

You are the team leader in your accounts department. The backlog of work cases increases by the day to the point that your colleagues are regularly missing weekly targets. You have to solve the issue before it escalates further.

What should you do?

> a. Remind your team of the problems and the clear need to meet every deadline.
>
> b. Communicate to your team that you are resolving the problems personally.
>
> c. Stay positive - and ask your immediate superior for additional resources.
>
> d. Meet with the team to tell them what you believe is causing the problems.

Scenario 40

You are new to a large company that uses software for supervision. Trying to cheat the software is a very serious crime that failing to report a colleague that cheats the system can land you in trouble. You discover 3 colleagues trying to cheat the system.

What should you do?

    a. Immediately report the three colleagues.

    b. Wait to see if they are good employees. Report them if they are lazy.

    c. Report them if they are absent on Friday.

    d. Look the other way as you have no evidence.

Scenario 41

As a department head, you propose new procedure and you are sure it will improve the work process. Some of the employee in the department oppose it. One of your subordinates criticizes the procedure to your direct boss.

What action should you take?

    a. You choose not to respond to prevent the situation to escalating into a conflict.

    b. You punish that person for skipping protocol and going to your boss and work to promote the idea more enthusiastically.

    c. You invite the employee for a discussion and explain to him that bypassing your authority cannot be tolerated.

    d. You decide to keep your employees satisfied by implementing the idea in part to maintain the employees trust in you as their manager.

Scenario 42

At a strategy meeting with your direct supervisor and the marketing manager, your find yourself in the middle of a conflict between them. You understand that the two are always in constant conflict and do not get along professionally. They are asking you to pick a side about the strategies for a new campaign.

What should you do?

> a. You go with the marketing managers idea since she is senior it would be safer and politically wiser to support her as she has more influence on the future of your career.
>
> b. You accept your supervisor's idea since he is directly above you and directly influences your daily routine which makes it politically correct to side with him.
>
> c. You measure the advantages and disadvantages of both sides and make a decision without getting involved in their personal conflict.
>
> d. You believe that choosing a side will negatively impact your career since both sides are superior to you. You refuse to pick a side and say both strategies are equally successful.

Scenario 43

After serving for two years as the sales manager, a new deputy manager is appointed by the director. You however find her disloyal and arrogant in many ways. You discover the director is considering an opportunity for her in a different position after this. The downside, is this would speed up her promotion.

What should you do?

a. Since she will eventually relocate, you encourage and approve her participation in the course.

b. You contact your director and recommend she be relocated to another position best suited to her capabilities.

c. You approve her participation and take time to discuss it with her. You honestly express your concerns and work out your differences and update your director.

d. You blindly approve her participation since it was offered by the director. You voice your concerns to the director separately.

Scenario 44

For the past year you have worked as a salesperson and have consistently hit sales targets. Recently, for personal reasons you haven't been focused and haven't been making sales targets. Changes in the market are also a factor, decreasing your sales by a significant margin. Your director does not seem to understand the changes in the market and is blaming you for the reduction in sales figures.

What should you do?

a. Talk to your director about your personal situation and apologize for the decline in the team's performance. Request for a few days off to put your house in order.

b. You decide to put your personal issues aside and consult other sales directors on how they deal with the changes in the market place. You fully dedicate yourself to your work.

c. You update your director on the market changes. You explain to him that changing or improving sales with the current conditions is beyond your ability.

d. You decide to put pressure on your team scolding them for the poor performance. You go ahead and set new targets with the market changes in mind.

Scenario 45

You have been working in the same company for 3 years and have successfully risen through the ranks. You now have the feeling that you have reached your potential in the company and start pursuing options to advance your career in other organizations. You are currently negotiating a new contract and rumors that you are switching jobs are spreading fast in your company.

What should you do?

a. You decide that since the rumor is already out, you update everyone of your ongoing negotiations in the new company. You do this as it may even push your current directors to give you a promotion in the current company.

b. Since nothing has been decided yet and it is still a rumor you maintain your silence on the issue until you give notice.

c. Since you will probably leave and the rumor is already out, you invest less and less in your current position and invest more time in getting the new position.

d. Since the rumor is out, you address your manager's doubts by updating him of your intentions of leaving and keep working normally since you are still an employee.

Scenario 46

The company you work for is having financial problems. You have come up with an innovative way to get more clients. The downside is the company will have to give up a loyal but less profitable client due to a conflict of interest. A few people on the marketing team agree with you, but your manager has a different opinion as he thinks the move is too risky.

What should you do?

a. You withdraw your proposition as you trust your managers judgement and believe there is no reason to go against his judgement.

b. You present a document that details the benefits your proposition will bring to the organization, but support his decision if he insists on it.

c. You implement the idea despite your managers resistance as you have a lot of faith in the proposition. You trust your gut and implement the idea behind your manager's back for the companies benefit.

d. You confront your manager and insist the idea is the best way out. You believe you are right you take the support of the marketing team and push your manager until he is convinced you are right.

Scenario 47

You are being undermined by a co-worker that has a junior position to you and has not been working there as long as you. He is, however, considered a fast learner and is more educated than you. You get information from someone that the co-worker is interested in taking over your some of your roles.

What should you do?

a. Wait to see how it turns out as all this is hearsay and you consider it rumors.

b. You call the co-worker and talk to them, letting them know that cooperation is essential in any organization and you have something to learn form each other. You say that you will take more serious action if he refuses to understand.

c. You treat the matter with seriousness taking no chances. Your report your co-worker to your supervisor and advise him to replace the co-worker.

d. Since you don't want to turn the matter into a big issue, you seek the help of a third party in telling your co-worker that their behavior cannot be tolerated.

Scenario 48

You are the manager of a department where two members are long overdue to participate in a professional training course. The training manager lets you know that she has opted for individuals from a different department for the training. You do not have a good relationship with the training department.

What should you do?

a. You reject the training manager's decision with a furious email demanding she re-opens the training as your employee's performance will be affected by their lack of training. You cc the email to the director.

b. You wait for the next training since your relationship with the training manager is already very poor.

c. You contact the manager of the other department and request a slot for one of your employees in the two slots he has been given.

d. You talk to the training manager to understand the reasons for her decision. You explain the importance of the training to your department and why it is necessary that your employee take it.

Scenario 49

One of your employees has shown significant decline in sales in the past month. Although this decline has been happening for a while, it has significantly increased in the past two weeks. In addition, the employee has been coming to work late and seems frustration in her work. Since she is a popular employee who has been working at the company for 2 years, her behavior is influencing the work atmosphere.

What should you do?

a. Explain to her that her behavior is not just affecting not only her performance, her but the entire office. You express your intentions to help her through whatever she's going through on condition she improves her attitude.

b. Since she is a popular employee you feel it necessary to replace her temporarily to prevent a decline in office performance. You assign her back office tasks and assure her she will have her role back if her performance improves.

c. You schedule a staff meeting to discus the negative attitude you in the office. You point out the problematic employee and talk about how she is affecting the office atmosphere hoping she will change.

d. You let it blow over. Since she has consistently proved to be a good employee you feel no need to reprimand her. Part of your job is to accommodate employees when they face challenging situations.

Scenario 50

You are assigned a joint project with a co-worker who has been working in the department longer than you have. He does not put in much effort as he lacks the motivation to develop professionally.

What should you do?

a. You accept the situation as it is and share the workload to the best of your ability. You leave the rest up to him.

b. You are concerned that poor quality work will effect your reputation and the company's reputation negatively and decide to put in extra hours to complete personally the project in the best way you can.

c. You contact your manger to report the situation as you cannot tolerate this attitude. You request the co-worker be replaced for the project.

d. You talk to the co-worker and negotiate that the work be distributed fairly between the two of you. You however consider the fact that you might have to put in extra effort to complete the project.

Scenario 51

You have been assigned the area with new products during a product launch.

What would you do to achieve exceptional customer experiences?

> a. Take a look at the display unit and conduct research on the products to get more informed
>
> b. Pass by the display unit to see what the products look like
>
> c. Check if your manager thinks it is beneficial to know more about the new stock
>
> d. Ask the colleague tomorrow morning to tell you about the new stock so that you can familiarize yourself

Scenario 52

You have just agreed to running product demos but you do not consider yourself an expert.

What should you do?

> a. Trust that you know enough to run the demo and ask for help if a customer needs more information
>
> b. Observe how others run the demo so that you can deliver the same customer service experience
>
> c. Have a quick catch up over lunch with a colleague knowledgeable about the product you will demo
>
> d. Agree to run the demo's today as best as you can but treat the opportunity as a learning experience

Scenario 53

You have been asked by a client take them to the shelves containing a particular item and recommend the best brand, you have little knowledge about the different brands.

What should you do?

a. Recommend the brand that you feel is more visually appealing

b. Suggest the customer talks to a more experienced colleague

c. Share with the client the little information you have on the brands

d. Ask an experienced colleague the share information on the brands and listen to gain experience

Scenario 54

Your store registered 2% of your customers to the company's loyalty scheme which was below the 12% target.

What would you do to increase performance?

a. Give a complementary discount to customers after subscribing to the loyalty scheme.

b. Ask you team to change the way they asked clients to sign up by making it more personal.

c. Ask every customer that you serve whether they would like to sign up.

d. Wait for customers to ask about the loyalty scheme and then encourage them to sign up.

Scenario 55

A client comes in late for an item that they have seen you have in stock. You are determined to close on time.

What should you do?

    a. Ask another colleague if they can stay and serve the customer as you feel exhausted

    b. Tell the customer where they can find the item but explain to them that another colleague will help

    c. Explain to the customer that the store is closing and check if you can help them in the morning

    d. Offer to help with their purchase but explain that the shop is closing in 10 minutes

Scenario 56

A customer requests that you help them take their package to the care but you have other clients waiting in line.

What should you do?

    a. Ask a colleague to serve the customers while you carry the items to the car park

    b. Politely explain that you need to serve the customers that have not received assistance

    c. Take the items to the customer's car quickly and get back to serving the other customers

    d. Of to look after the customers items so they don't have to carry everything at once

Scenario 57

A client has come back with a complaint that they were given the wrong item but you were not on duty when he was served.

What should you do?

> a. Ask for the part of the order that were incorrect and pass the information to your colleague
>
> b. Offer to get the colleague they spoke to so that the situation can be clarified
>
> c. Find out which part of the order were incorrect and check whether the products he wanted are available
>
> d. Explain that mistakes happen and ask if they would like a refund on the products

Scenario 58

You have noticed that you are running low on a particular product. Your colleagues feel you have enough to last your shift but the store will be open for 3 more hours after your shift.

What should you do?

> a. Listen to your colleague but ask them to get more stock if you run out of the item.
>
> b. Explain why you think the stock is low and why it is important to maintain stock levels for customers
>
> c. Continue serving and customers and let someone else get more if the product runs out after your shift
>
> d. Stop what you are doing and collect more stock to ensure there's enough for the whole day.

Scenario 59

A client has come for one of your best sellers but it is out of stock. You have informed them you think it is out of stock.

What else can you do?

> a. Recommend a suitable alternative so that you can make the sale
>
> b. Suggest a different store even if they are not part of your company
>
> c. Offer to check the stock in other store locations for home delivery
>
> d. Explain that the product was really popular and you're sorry it is not in stock at the moment

Scenario 60

Your phone completely breaks down while talking to client leaving them hanging.

What should you do?

> a. Email your manager informing them of the situation and ask what they would do.
>
> b. Call the customer from your personal phone, apologizing that they were cut-off
>
> c. Send the customer an email and ask if they can talk to you using a live communication platform.
>
> d. Get a colleague to call the customer on your behalf and ask them to explain the situation.

Answer Key

1. A
By motivating him, you positively impact the results. Everyone needs a pat in the back and a person to motivate them when tough times comes.

Choice B, informing the supervisors, might not be the most appropriate thing to do, at least at first. As a colleague, its incorrect to do absolutely nothing (choice D). If motivating fails, you may then suggest counseling sessions (choice C).

2. A
The first impression is important in human encounters because it lasts through the duration the people get to interact. Good posture and clothing are indicators of success and the clients are likely to trust you more.

Choice C, dramatizing your idea does not necessarily mean that you create a good first impression. Choices B and D, ignoring the advice is no solution.

3. B
Insisting on a plan to minimize the potential risk will save the team from potential problems without involving anyone outside the team.

4. B
We all get bored easily by routine. By finding new tasks to engage, you trick the brain in staying active for longer periods of time.

Winners never quit, that is the basic principle in any form of business. As an employee, you shouldn't focus on getting a simpler job. Instead, your focus should be on building capacity to withstand and overcome challenges.

5. A
Introducing incentives is likely to motivate your team members. Choice B, reducing compensation is likely to alienating. Choice C, talking about the need to be committed could easily come across as talking down. Choice D, is not realistic.

While compensating the employees who perform exemplary, one creates unnecessary competition zones which could in turn be bad for business.

6. A
Complimenting him in public, you motivate other employees to do better. This is a sure way to increase their level of commitment to the success of the business.

Choice B, demeaning others will reduce moral and motivation. Choice C, emailling may be the only option under some circumstances but not the best.

7. A
Regular meetings keep everyone up-to-date to discuss issues, potential improvements and in touch.

Choice B will not help. Choice C, selecting the best team players, means re-making the whole team – only as a last resort. Choice D, becoming more involved is good advice, but choice A is better.

8. B
If you want the best, you need to become the best. By working longer hours, you encourage your team members. Choice A is good, but choice B is better because it is more visible. Everyone will you arriving early and leaving late. Lecturing or condemning, choices C and D, never helps.

9. B
Making clear to the team the deadlines and what is expected of them is the first step.

Choice C is a good suggestion, if there is an issue with some parts of the project.

10. A
Making clear to the team the deadlines and what is expected and so everyone knows where they stand.

Choice B, keeping a monopoly of information is likely to cause chaos and lead to disruption. Working three times harder, choice C, however effective it may sound, is equally ineffective.

11. B
Communication is especially important in business environments. Being attentive while communicating you can avoid confusion and misinterpretation. Clear communication leads to better performance.

Although it sounds quite okay to practice yoga, choice A, not all employees understand what it is or the benefits and may not be interested.

12. A
Everybody wants to feel important. By ensuring that the employees feel involved, you keep morale and productivity up. Leadership styles vary greatly but the sure thing is being bossy to employees leads to reduced productivity. Asserting control or dictating makes people defensive and resist.

13. C
This is a challenging situation and getting everyone on board to solve is very important.

Choices A, B and D, are moving ahead blindly.

14. A
People buy things because they want the benefits. This is the only way to convince someone to buy.

The other choices, increasing pressure (hard-sell as choice B) ignoring objections, (choice C) don't work in the long term.

15. C
You are being blamed, and fair or not this is the reality. The first step is to strategize. Maybe this can be solved with a new strategy and maybe not.

Blaming the supervisor back doesn't solve the problem (choice A). Going over the supervisor's head, choice B, maybe a good strategy for your next step, but not initially.

16. A
It's important to make your side of the story known as a way to avoid confusion and misinterpretation.

By blaming and accusing others you don't help yourself.

17. A
The first step in dealing with difficult people is to stay calm and understand their point of view.

After that you can start to build rapport.

Choice C, reporting to your supervisor you can't work with them may be a second step but basically doesn't solve the problem. Choice D, ignoring their unhelpful behavior, depends on how serious it is – if it is minor this may be OK.

However, Choice A, is the best choice because you are going to have to get along with them.

18. D
The best thing with failure is the lessons it brings. By encouraging him or her to learn from their mistakes, you give them the chance to improve.

Choice A, criticizing does nothing to improving their situation. The person criticized will in turn find fault in you and blame you. Focus on the issues that bring success to the business.

19. D
Everyone wants to feel part of something and involved. As an employee your options are limited.

Training is great, (choice A) but as an employee you probably won't be able to. Rebelling, choice C, isn't going to change the situation.

20. A
It is important therefore to refer your colleague to a guidance session where he can get the appropriate assistance.

Comparing their problems with yours, Choice B, will not make them feel any better or be able to perform better. Reporting this matter to the supervisor, choice C, could solve the problem, but also could bring problems to your colleague and worsen their condition. Unless you have been trained on how to handle stress-related issues, then it's not advisable to give counseling sessions to a person who shows signs of distress. It could accomplish quite the opposite.

21. B
This problem should be handled immediately and talking to your colleague addresses the urgency. This will also give the colleague a chance to change if what she did was genuinely by mistake.

22. D
Discussing the patient's home circumstances with his general practitioner before making any promises to him is the right thing to do. This will help you avoid giving false promises to the patient if his home circumstances are not conducive for his condition. The general practitioner will also advise on the right time to take him home.

23. B
Response B will be the right thing to say to the client. First you need to apologize for failing to deliver the package on time. Show integrity by giving the reason why the package has not been delivered without justification. The response also reassures the client that the package will be delivered.

24. D
Before selling a product, you need to have a feel of how the product works. This can only happen if you try out the product yourself. Familiarizing with the product will enable you understand how it operates and be able to address objections that might be raised by customers effectively.

25. D
Helping the colleague and finding a future remedy will save the current situation and provide a long-term solution.

26. B
Reporting the error to your senior is the right thing to do.

27. A
This will help the colleague understand the importance of respecting protocol.

28. B
Offering to go out of your way to ensure the customer gets what they wanted.

Choices A, C and D are incorrect. They do not address the issue in the most appropriate way.

29. B
Asking for permission is the right thing as you will be given ample time to tidy up.

30. D
Choice D is the best approach - a proactive approach.

31. A
Choice A is the best solution.

32. C
Talking to staff will help you uncover the root cause for the poor team morale.

33. A
Using 1-on-1's will open opportunities for each individual to work with their abilities.

34. B
Input from more experienced team members will solve the problem without sounding like you are shutting anyone down.

The other choices, A, C and D will make the junior colleague feel attacked.

35. B
Introducing a half-hour, weekly catch-up meeting will help people feel comfortable around each other and encourage conversations.

The other choices, A, C and D, are imposed solutions and will not be fully accepted.

36. D
This will help the intern know what to concentrate on in their future reports.

The other choices, A, B and C do offer long-term solutions.

37. B
this will save everyone's time as the entire team is paying little attention to the presentation.

The other choices, A, C and D do not provide solutions that will benefit the entire team.

38. A
Senior team members can handle the matter in the most appropriate manner.

The other choices, B, C and D may escalate the situation.

39. C
Requesting additional resources will go a long way in enabling your team work better.

CHoices A, B and D will not solve the situation.

40. A
This is the right thing to do. Failing to report might also land you in trouble.

The other choices are all against the company policy.

41. C
Going over your head is disrespectful of your authority. Even though the new idea will make their work easier, some employees are resistant to change. Inviting them for a discussion demonstrates that you are serious about the idea and that you are available for discussions in case of a problem.

Ignoring the mistake, choice A, to avoid conflict will send a signal that you fear conflict. Punishing the employee, choice B, will probably cause resentment.

42. C
As a professional, you need to rise above personal conflict, even if others are not. Giving a professional opinion and risk going into the bad books of one of your superiors demonstrates that you are ready to risk personal gratification for the team's success.

Refusing to pick a side, or picking a side based on politics, might be a safe option to choose to a short-cited individual.

This will not serve the organizational and both the manager and supervisor will be able to read your weakness in decision making. It will be clear to them you cannot make a decision for the benefit of the company.

43. C
This scenario has shown us that the deputy director is not incompetent but is arrogant and disloyal. This course will only improve her academic qualification but will not address he arrogance and disloyalty. Talking to her will open up her mind to her weaknesses and give her a chance to reflect on them and correct. Informing the director will enable him find a solution to her weaknesses and find a way of helping her without compromising the company goals.

Approving her application without talking to her, (choice A) will only shift the problem from your department to the department she will be transferred to. Talking to the director without trying to address the issue first,(choice D), will not help her as she might lose the opportunity.

44. B
One should not allow their personal life to affect their professional life. To effectively cope with a volatile market, consult more experienced salespeople.

45. D
It is the responsibility of the employee to inform their manager of their intention to leave. This will help the manager in planning for the future. It will also give the manager a chance to address issues that might have caused you to look elsewhere for employment. It is also important to continue working normally as you are still an employee of the company you work for.

46. B
You need to try to convince the manager by educating him on the benefits of the idea backed by evidence without arguing with him in the presence of his subordinates. You also have a duty and obligation to support whatever decision the manager makes even if you believe you have a better idea.

47. B
By choosing choice B you will show honesty and genuine interest in the issue at hand. This serves the purpose of educating your co-worker on the benefits of cooperation. It is fair to take more action if the co-worker chooses to ignore your advice.

48. D
Choice D is the most effective. This might even give you a chance to sort out your strained relationship.

49. A
By selecting choice A as a manager, you have decided to solve the problem in a proactive way. Addressing the problem by talking to the employee will assure her that you care. As an employee that has consistently performed well talking to her will enable the manager get a better understanding of the problem she is facing and better help her.

Calling a staff meeting to address a personal problem, choice C, is a waste of time and a counter productive move. Publicly reprimanding a popular employee will only worsen the situation as she might feel offended. The employee might turn resentful and the hope that the behavior will improve might never come.

50. D
A joint project requires teamwork and team work requires communication and constant negotiation on what should be done and how it should be done. Negotiating and distributing the work fairly between the two of you will ensure he steps up and takes responsibility for his part of the project. However, because of the situation and poor performance will reflect badly on you as well, be prepared to put in some extra.

51. A
Conducting research about the products will go a long way in boosting your confidence and customer service.

52. A
Confidence will help you deliver great customer experience.

53. D
It will serve the client's need and add to your experience

54. B
This approach will convince customers to sign up without bribing them.

55. D
It gives the client a chance to be served by you.

56. A
The other customers will be served, and this customer will be helped.

57. C
This solves the problem without throwing your colleague under the bus.

58. B
Explaining the importance of maintaining stock levels will enable your colleagues make sense of what you are saying.

59. B
This assists the customer and they will appreciate it.

60. D
A colleague will be able to sort out the customer's problem.

Conclusion

Congratulations! You have made it this far because you have applied yourself diligently to practicing for the exam and no doubt improved your potential score considerably! Getting into a good school is a huge step in a journey that might be challenging at times but will be many times more rewarding and fulfilling. That is why being prepared is so important.

Study then Practice and then Succeed!

Good Luck!

Register for Free Updates and More Practice Test Questions

Register your purchase at
https://www.test-preparation.ca/register/

for updates, free test tips and more practice test questions.

https://www.facebook.com/CompleteTestPreparation/

https://www.youtube.com/user/MrTestPreparation

Online Resources

How to Prepare for a Test - The Ultimate Guide

https://www.test-preparation.ca/prepare-test/

Learning Styles - The Complete Guide

https://www.test-preparation.ca/learning-style/

Test Anxiety Secrets!

https://www.test-preparation.ca/test-anxiety/

Time Management on a Test

https://www.test-preparation.ca/time-management/

Flash Cards - The Complete Guide

https://www.test-preparation.ca/flash-cards/

Test Preparation Video Series

https://www.test-preparation.ca/test-video/

How to Memorize - The Complete Guide

https://www.test-preparation.ca/memorize/

Online Library of Student Tips and Strategies

https://www.test-preparation.ca/students-say/

www.ingramcontent.com/pod-product-compliance
Lightning Source LLC
Chambersburg PA
CBHW071907070526
44583CB00016B/1884